NATIONAL GEOGRAPHIC

Ladders

African Savanna

SO-AEW-541

Elephant Orphanage

by Suzanne Sherman

Four-year-old Kilaguni rushes toward Kibo, a three-year-old. They playfully wrap their trunks together before bumping heads. Then, at the sound of their keeper preparing a bottle, Kilaguni and Kibo break for a midday feeding.

Both Kibo and Kilaguni came to the David Sheldrick Wildlife Trust's elephant nursery in Kenya when they were just infants. Kibo was two weeks old when he was found trapped in a well. Kilaguni was six months old when he was brought to the nursery with injuries to his tail and ears. Their mothers were nowhere to be found. Through the Wildlife Trust's Orphans' Project, young African elephants that are injured and orphaned can heal and grow into healthy adults.

The nursery provides the elephants with food, shelter, and relationships, which are key to their survival. Elephants are highly social animals that can't survive without a family. In the wild, young elephants are raised by the females of their families. Elephants form strong bonds within these groups that last their whole lives, up to 70 years. An elephant is so close to its family that it seems to show grief when a member dies.

Each elephant in the orphanage has its own personality. For some, the stress of losing their family can cause the elephant to act out. But most of the elephants make a full recovery with the help of other orphaned elephants and caring humans.

Social bonds are key to an elephant's well-being.

Where Are the Adults?

More than a million elephants once roamed the continent of Africa. Now there are only about 500,000 elephants. People have taken much of the elephants' land for farming. People also **poach**, or illegally kill, elephants for meat, to protect their crops from trampling, or for greed. Many people want objects made from ivory, such as this carving, which has led to a rise in elephant poaching.

ELEPHANT POPULATION DECLINE

Less than half a century ago, there were an estimated 1.3 million African elephants. Habitat loss and poaching has brought the number down to around 500,000.

1979

Elephant tusks are taken from poachers and burned. That shows the government's resolve to end poaching.

Tens of thousands of elephants are poached for their tusks each year. In 1989, a worldwide ban was placed on ivory trade. The ban seemed to be working. Some wild elephant herds began to make a comeback. But ivory from elephants that died of natural causes could still be sold. In China, Thailand, and the Philippines, ivory is carved into religious statues and charms. The value of these religious objects has made the price of ivory soar. Now, greedy dealers buy and sell any ivory they can get, even if it means elephants were poached for it. The law against poaching is difficult to enforce and many get away with breaking it.

Elephant tusks are incisor teeth that continue to grow over the course of the elephant's life. Males and females use tusks mostly for defense. Poachers seek out adult elephants since their tusks can be up to six feet long. This leaves many young elephants to care for themselves— such as many of the orphans of the Wildlife Trust.

2012

One white elephant represents 100,000 elephants in the wild.

Growing Up

Raising elephants in the Orphans' Project is a three-part process. From the nursery, the elephants progress to a rehabilitation center, and then begin the transition back into the wild. Baby elephants depend on their mothers' milk for the first two years of life. In the nursery, human keepers feed the baby elephants with large bottles. It took the project's founder, Daphne Sheldrick, and her husband decades to get the ingredients for the milk formula just right.

Human keepers and fellow elephants create a surrogate family for the orphans. Older female elephants especially enjoy looking after the younger ones. Keepers stay with the babies 24 hours a day. They feed the elephants, keep them warm with blankets, and give them plenty of time for social play. At night, keepers even sleep next to them. Keepers sleep next to different elephants each night so the elephants don't attach to just one person.

Caring nursery keepers act as stand-ins for the baby elephants' family members.

When the orphans no longer depend only on milk, they are moved to one of two rehabilitation centers in Tsavo East National Park. At this stage, the keepers start taking them out to the bush. There, elephants learn to nibble on natural vegetation to supplement their milk diet. But vegetation is not the only thing the orphans discover in the wild. There they will meet wild elephants for the first time.

Daphne Sheldrick

Back Into the Wild

The final step of the Orphans' Project is the reintroduction of the elephants into the wild. This happens only when an orphan chooses a wild family to join and decides to leave for good. The elephants are torn between joining the wild group and leaving their orphanage family. They will often leave and come back many times. It may be eight to ten years before the elephants are fully wild again.

The Orphan's Project has been very successful. Most of the orphans that survive recover and grow to become healthy adults. So far, more than a hundred elephants have been returned to the wild.

Orphan and wild elephants mingle over a fence.

And they come back to visit! Elephants are known for their great memories, so they never forget their keepers. One female came back to visit the keepers many years after living in the wild. She wanted to show them her new baby!

At the time of this writing, Kibo and Kilaguni are thriving in the rehabilitation center. Kilaguni can drink on his own by holding the bottle with his trunk. Years from now, when they are ready, Kibo and Kilaguni will once again roam the African **savanna.**

Check In Why aren't young elephants released into the wild as soon as their wounds are healed?

Living on the AF

by Suzanne Sherman

Over a million wildebeests migrate north from Tanzania to Kenya and back each year.

In the heat of the African **savanna**, the baking earth has been trampled over thousands of years. Streams have been drying for weeks, the grasses turning brown. A steady, booming sound fills the air, getting louder and louder. It is the pounding of millions of wildebeests' hooves as the animals make their way across the African savanna. These large, horned mammals travel a thousand miles each year in search of fresh water to drink and green grass to graze on.

The African savanna **ecosystem** has wet and dry seasons. An ecosystem includes all of the organisms in an area as well as conditions such as temperature and rainfall. During the wet season, rivers flood. During the dry season, lakes dry out. Plants and animals on the African

Savanna covers almost half the surface of Africa.

savanna have adapted to extreme heat and periods of drought. Some, such as insects and meerkats, go underground to escape the heat. Others, such as wildebeests, elephants, and zebras, migrate in the dry season.

Tall grasses die back during the dry season, but their tiny buds stay alive near the surface of the soil. Acacia trees have deep roots that find water. The trees' small, waxy leaves help store the little water the trees have.

The living things of the African savanna are richly connected. For example, as the wildebeests cross the land, they cut the grasses and fertilize the soil with their droppings. They also provide food for the crocodiles, lions, and cheetahs. Connections such as these allow a surprising number of species to survive here.

MEET the WILDLIFE

The African savanna ecosystem is home to some of the most incredible plants and animals on the planet.

cheetah

zebra

baobab

secretary bird

white rhinoceros

black mamba

termite mound

acacia

giraffe

red grass

CHEETAH A cheetah's spotted coat helps it blend into the dry grasses as it follows its prey. This runner can reach 96 km/h (60 mph) in three seconds!

ACACIA Tall acacia trees provide much-needed shade on the savanna. Pairs of long, sharp thorns keep most animals from munching on its leaves.

GIRAFFE The giraffe's purple tongue is tough enough to take the leaves off acacia trees without a scratch. Giraffes give the trees an umbrella shape as they eat the lowest leaves.

ZEBRA The pattern of stripes on a zebra can confuse its predators. Each zebra's pattern is unique, like a fingerprint.

BAOBAB The baobab tree stores water for the dry season in its trunk. Its small leaves limit water loss, and its thick bark protects it from fire.

RED GRASS Red grass is food for grazers on the savanna. The long bristles of its flower twirl when wet, and its seeds flutter to the ground.

SECRETARY BIRD The tall feathers on the head of a secretary bird look like the quill pens that secretaries used to use. These birds pant to keep cool in the heat.

WHITE RHINOCEROS White rhinos are really tan or gray. They keep cool by bathing in mud, a natural sunblock and bug repellent.

BLACK MAMBA Black mambas are among the world's fastest snakes and are also among the deadliest. Their lethal venom can kill any animal.

TERMITE MOUND Termite mounds, built over centuries from mud and termite saliva, help aerate the savanna soil. Lions and cheetahs use termite mounds as lookout points. Small animals on the savanna use them for shade.

FOOD for ALL

The story of life in the African savanna ecosystem truly begins with the sun. In only about eight minutes, energy travels from the sun to Earth. There, it fuels one living thing after another in a series of feeding relationships called a **food chain.**

Sunlight energy hits the leaf of an acacia tree. The tree is a **producer,** so it uses the energy to make its own food. Some of the energy is stored but the tree may never get to use it. Along comes an elephant, a **consumer** that cannot make its own food. The elephant eats the leaves and uses the tree's stored energy for its own survival.

The African savanna has the most types of herbivores, or plant-eating consumers, in the world. Grazers eat low plants and grasses while browsers eat from trees and shrubs. Elephants, wildebeests, zebras,

GRASS
producer

HYENA
consumer

rhinos, giraffes, and warthogs are all herbivores of the savanna.

A female lion stalks an injured elephant as the other members of her team silently close in. Suddenly, they take the elephant down. Lions, leopards, cheetahs, and wild dogs are all carnivores of the savanna. These consumers get all their energy by eating other animals.

Scavengers get their energy from eating dead animals. Hyenas, vultures, and jackals are scavengers of the savanna. Decomposers, such as bacteria and fungi, use the remaining energy. Decomposers break down any leftovers and release nutrients into the soil.

This chain is just one possible path energy can take through the savanna ecosystem. All the different food chains make up a **food web.**

TREES and SHRUBS
producers

VULTURE
consumer

ELEPHANT
consumer

LION
consumer

TEAM WORK

Think of all the savanna interactions you have read about so far. These relationships are an important part of the savanna ecosystem. Some species of the African savanna have joined forces to form unusual partnerships.

warthog + mongoose

The ugly mug of this warthog does not deter a group of banded mongooses. The warthog lies down and mongooses come running. They climb all over the warthog's skin and eat insects that the warthog would not be able to clear away by itself.

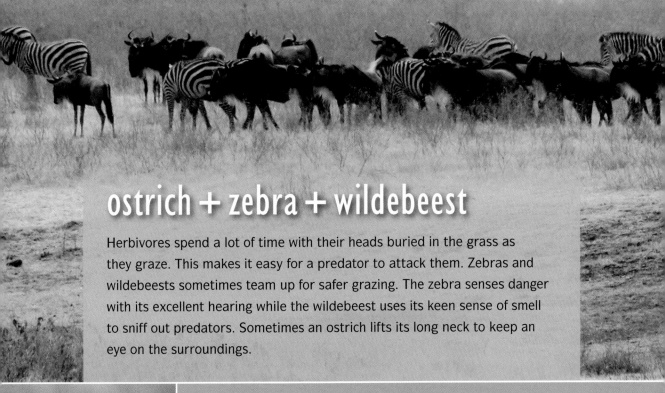

ostrich + zebra + wildebeest

Herbivores spend a lot of time with their heads buried in the grass as they graze. This makes it easy for a predator to attack them. Zebras and wildebeests sometimes team up for safer grazing. The zebra senses danger with its excellent hearing while the wildebeest uses its keen sense of smell to sniff out predators. Sometimes an ostrich lifts its long neck to keep an eye on the surroundings.

giraffe + oxpecker

A giraffe and red-billed oxpeckers form an unlikely team. The oxpeckers get a meal of ticks and insects. The giraffe gets cleaned of pests. If a predator approaches while the giraffe is sleeping, the oxpeckers chirp and flap their wings to wake it.

Check In Explain three different strategies that wildlife use to survive on the savanna.

LOOK AROUND

the room you're in—the walls, the floor, the furniture. All of it was created by people. We cause great change to our **ecosystem** when we build structures, but we are not the only living things that change our environment. Some animals build surprisingly complex homes. Male weaver birds build detailed nests, hoping to attract females with their artistic skill and creativity.

WOVEN HOMES

The village weaver is a noisy and colorful bird. It builds its nests on trees near rivers and streams in the African **savanna** and other places. The nests are woven out of leaves, grasses, and reeds. Sometimes more than a hundred nests dangle from one tree. When the male finishes building the nest, he advertises his work to females. He hangs upside down, flutters his wings, and chatters loudly.

A male village weaver shows off his creation.

Animal A

by Suzanne Sherman

A social weaver nest may have up to 100 entrances. They are located at the bottom of the nest.

The social weaver builds a giant nest in an acacia tree. As many as 400 birds may live in one apartment-style nest. Each family has its own entrance that leads to its own sleeping area. A thick roof holds in heat at night and keeps the nest cool in the day.

Sometimes an African pygmy falcon will make its home in one of the rooms of a social weaver nest. The falcon acts like a security guard as it feeds on reptiles that prey on the birds. In return, the falcon gets a "rent-free" apartment.

rchitects

SWEET DIGS

Under the ground in Eastern Africa, lives an odd little animal known as the naked mole rat. These rodents have no ears and almost no eyes. They live their whole lives in tunnels underground. They have fine hairs on their bodies that act like whiskers to help them feel their surroundings. Using these hairs to "see," they can run backward through their tunnels as well as forward.

Naked mole rats use their long front teeth to dig burrows large enough to house hundreds of family members. A network of tunnels connects a variety of rooms. In a nursery, the queen tends to the pups. In a kitchen, food is stored and eaten. There is even a bathroom! Although the above-ground temperature varies, the temperature inside the burrow stays at 30°C (86°F).

The naturalist who first discovered the naked mole rat thought it was diseased because of its lack of fur.

THE NAKED TRUTH

Naked mole rats are not actually moles or rats. They are related to porcupines, chinchillas, and guinea pigs.

Naked mole rats live in large colonies with a queen, soldiers, and workers.

When digging, several naked mole rats will line up in a row. They sweep the dirt back like a conveyer belt.

Naked mole rats have no sweat glands to help them cool off or insulating fat to keep them warm.

Naked mole rats don't get cancer. Scientists are working to understand why.

The skin of a naked mole rat doesn't sense pain.

Naked mole rats live up to 28 years, which is longer than any other rodent.

Check In   How do the homes of the weaver bird and naked mole rat help them survive in the African savanna climate?

SAVING BIG CATS

by Suzanne Sherman

BEVERLY AND DERECK JOUBERT are award-winning wildlife photographers, filmmakers, and conservationists. They are also National Geographic Explorers. They have observed and documented African wildlife for nearly 30 years. They have produced nature films and books. Beverly Joubert took most of the photos on the following pages.

Beverly and Dereck Joubert document big cats and other African animals. Their goal is to capture the lives of these animals in their natural environment and to help others understand and appreciate them.

The Jouberts take care not to disturb the animals they are documenting. If there is nothing to shoot, they must wait. Not only does this work take patience, it also takes courage. They have had to swim through crocodile-infested water, face an angry elephant, and watch out for all kinds of dangerous creatures.

The Jouberts believe the rewards and challenges of their work help them honestly show what animal life is like in Africa. In 2003, the Jouberts met an eight-day-old leopard in Botswana. They followed her as she grew, learned to hunt, and parted with her mother. This leopard, which they named Legadema, or "light from the sky," taught them an important lesson: conservation is about individual animals with lives and personalities.

A mother leopard grooms her cub.

Launching an Initiative

Dereck and Beverly have observed all kinds of big cats in the wild. They understand lions as well as anyone could. And they know the future of the lion is in great danger.

In the last 50 years, the population of lions in Africa has dropped from 450,000 to only around 20,000. If lions continue to decline at this rate, they will be gone from the wild forever. People are the reason. A growing population of humans is destroying the lions' habitat. **Poaching** is also a major threat to lions. Cattle herders also kill lions to defend their livestock.

Since people have caused the lions' downfall, the Jouberts believe that people can bring them back.

The Jouberts' mission is the conservation of large cats and other key wildlife in Africa. One way they help is by working with Great Plains Conservation, a company that buys large areas of land in Africa to preserve the big cats' habitat.

Together with National Geographic, the Jouberts have started the Big Cats Initiative. The goal is to save the big cats in Africa and elsewhere before they are gone for good. The Big Cats Initiative raises awareness and funding to support conservation.

The Jouberts' vehicle is also their studio, office, kitchen, and sleeping quarters.

Why Big Cats Matter

As top predators, lions are a **keystone species.** Like a center stone that supports an arch, a keystone species supports the rest of the **ecosystem.** Top predators such as big cats keep populations of grazers in check. As big cats follow grazers, they drive their migration. If grazers overpopulate the land and stop migrating, the plants and soil would be affected. All the other animals that depend on the plants and soil would be affected, too.

Top predators are necessary to the health of an ecosystem. How do we know? Just look at Yellowstone National Park in the United States for evidence. Gray wolves are a keystone species of the Yellowstone ecosystem. After they were killed off by American settlers in the 1800s, everything changed. Without wolves to hunt them, the elk were no longer afraid to stand out in the open and graze on trees.

Trees near stream edges disappeared, and as a result, other animals lost their habitat. The removal of one species—the gray wolf—affected the entire ecosystem. This top predator has since been reintroduced to the Yellowstone ecosystem and the natural ecosystem has made a comeback. Big cats are likely to be just as important to the African **savanna** ecosystem.

Local communities need top predators, too. Tourists from around the world come to see lions and cheetahs. The ecotourism industry brings in $80 billion a year, and a large portion of that goes to African communities. Without big cats drawing in the tourists, the money would be lost.

Traditional fences leave Maasai livestock open to attack. In another Big Cat Initiative program, Maasai are provided with improved fencing to keep predators out.

Finding Peace

One Big Cat Initiative program is working to improve the relationship between the Maasai people of Kenya and lions. The Maasai have lived in East Africa for hundreds of years. Cattle are central to Maasai life. The people protect, feed, and care for the cattle. In return, the cattle provide milk and blood for food and hides for mattresses and shoes. The cattle are traded with other groups for clothes, food, and school. To the Maasai, cattle are wealth, and they are viewed as a sacred gift.

Maasai houses are temporary structures built of sticks and cattle dung. The people often travel in search of the best pasture for their livestock. This often takes them near Kenya's parks and reserves, where lions and other predators live.

A Maasai herder uses a radio receiver to track the activity of lions.

The pens the Maasai build for their livestock do not offer much protection. Many cattle and goats fall prey to lions. In turn, the Maasai kill the lions. This has caused lion numbers in the Maasai region to drop to below 200.

The Maasai depend on their cattle to subsist, so the Big Cat Initiative program gives money to herders who have lost livestock to lions.

The program also pays the Maasai to protect the lions. Many lions in the region have been fitted with radio collars. The Maasai use receivers to keep track of the lions' activity.

Using cell phones, they tell other herders where to guide their livestock, and alert authorities when they spot hunters. Far fewer lions have been killed in the area since the program began.

Making a Movie

While watching big cats, Beverly and Dereck Joubert have seen complex relationships and struggles for survival. They've seen death, but they have also seen animals survive against all odds.

When we appreciate the life of another creature, we reflect on our own: our own ability to overcome life's struggles, our own relationships, and our own thoughts on life and death.

For three decades, the Jouberts have shared their concern for big cats through films. In 2011, they launched *The Last Lions: An Incredible True Story of Survival*. As a result of this movie, they hope to raise awareness, support, and funding for Big Cat Initiative projects.

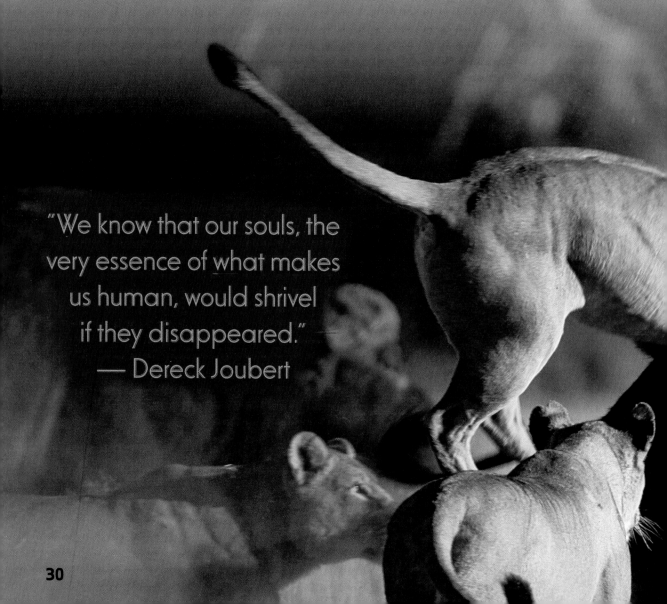

"We know that our souls, the very essence of what makes us human, would shrivel if they disappeared."
— Dereck Joubert

The movie is a suspense-filled tale of a lioness they named, Ma di Tau, or "Mother of Lions." Ma di Tau bravely faces challenges as she struggles to keep herself and her cubs alive.

Although deeply beautiful, the movie is not meant to be a celebration of lions. Its purpose is to honestly portray what may truly be the last of the wild lions. *The Last Lions* is the Jouberts' call to action.

According to the Jouberts, losing Africa's big cats would mean more than losing a wild animal and its ecosystem. It would mean losing an animal that has been a symbol of bravery and strength for people for thousands of years.

Check In How do you think the Jouberts' film can make a difference to the big cats?

Discuss

1. What connections can you make among the four pieces in this book?

2. Think about and describe two ways people affect African elephants.

3. What effects might wildebeests have on the savanna ecosystem if all the big cats were killed off?

4. What are the main producers of the African savanna? Why are they called producers?

5. Describe some ways social weaver birds interact with living and nonliving things in their environment.

6. What else do you want to learn about the African savanna? How could you learn more?